THEN & NOW

CHARLOTTE

Opposite: J and D Tires, "Made in Charlotte," sponsored this Charlotte parade float *c.* 1920. McClaren Rubber Company manufactured J and D Tires on West Palmer Street. Trolley No. 45 can be seen in the background. The lettering on its side reads "Southern Public Utilities Co." Until it was absorbed by Duke Power Company, Southern Public Utilities owned the trolley line. Notice also the classic "Diamond T" truck from which the float was fashioned.

CHARLOTTE

Don Schick

For Hannah, who is my inspiration, and who I am sure will make some history of her own one day. I love you, Sweetheart.

Library of Congress control number: 2005933695

Published by Arcadia Publishing
Charleston SC, Chicago IL, Portsmouth NH, San Francisco CA

For all general information contact Arcadia Publishing at:
Telephone 843-853-2070
Fax 843-853-0044
E-mail sales@arcadiapublishing.com
For customer service and orders:
Toll-Free 1-888-313-2665

Visit us on the internet at www.arcadiapublishing.com

On the Front Cover: Perhaps no two images in this volume better exemplify Charlotte's evolution than the two on the front cover. Notwithstanding the particular changes—the cars, the attire, and the signs—the more striking changes would seem to be the overall landscape and the walks of life that frequent this location. On the other hand, one could argue that the people have changed little. A closer look reveals that each view depicts much of the same: men and women, young and old, and black and white. If nothing else, these views are a commentary on the cocktail of personalities, ethnicities, and backgrounds that make American cities what they are.

On the Back Cover: The College Street Garage, shown *c.* 1913, operated at 223 North College Street. Advertising Ford maintenance as a specialty, the College Street Garage is thought to be Charlotte's first Ford repairs facility. The garage also sold gasoline. Fittingly Fuel Pizza is on this site today at the base of the Hearst Tower. Fuel is a chain of gasoline-themed pizza parlors throughout the city.

CONTENTS

ACKNOWLEDGMENTS

Words fail to truly capture the debt of gratitude owed to all those without whom the completion of this book would not have been possible. From the outset of this undertaking, the author sought assistance from many and received with regularity much more help than was ever anticipated.

Angela Ritter, who is responsible for all of the modern images in this volume, is a young architect for the Charlotte firm Liquid Design, and she contributed as much in research as photography. Her tireless efforts, willingness to confer with the author on an almost daily basis, and never-ending enthusiasm for the project quite simply made this book far more than it ever would have been without her involvement. The very idea of meeting deadlines without her assistance is pure fantasy. She deserves particular credit for determining the site of Bob's Esso Station after spending the better part of an evening driving up and down Central Avenue searching for clues to its location.

Listed second but providing equally invaluable aid, the staff at the Robinson-Spangler Carolina Room of the Charlotte-Mecklenburg Public Library is a human treasure to the city of Charlotte. They are, alphabetically: Gerri Blenman, Shelia Bumgarner, Valerie Burnie, Jane Johnson, Rosemary Lands, and Joyce Reimann. As a staff, these ladies have extraordinary personal knowledge of Charlotte history and immeasurable knowledge of the paths to researching the topic.

Photograph Librarian Shelia Bumgarner has the author's sincerest thanks for providing virtually all of the vintage photographs in this volume from the library's collection. A request for images or information—there were dozens of each—was never met with anything short of complete and total willingness to provide what was needed, and enthusiasm to provide more than was asked. Most impressive was her acceptance of the author's deadlines as her own.

The list of individuals who contributed along the way is long. Two that offered direction from the outset of the project are Babak Emadi, principal of Urbana Architecture, and Kelly Herr, office manager of Meca Properties. Without their suggestions and guidance, this endeavor may well have ground to a halt long before the help of the others listed above was recruited.

Finally and most important of all, the author wishes to thank Hannah, who cheerfully tolerated her father's fatigue in the closing weeks before this book's completion.

INTRODUCTION

Charlotte, North Carolina, is a city that's supplanted a town by the same name. As finance mixed with industry, Northerners with Southerners, and the urbane with the "salt of the earth," Charlotte was stirred into a cultural cocktail. Today that cultural, and in turn architectural, tug-of-war rages on—the ever-emerging city pulls one end of history, the town pulls the other. The city is winning.

The intent of this volume is to span that gap, not just between town and city, but between generations of citizens who hold this place in common, if not much else. Life-long Charlotteans are invited to recall the simpler place where they were raised, the streets they walked, the businesses they supported, and perhaps even the homes they inhabited. Tens of thousands of Charlotte transplants are asked to view the Charlotte they know and merely to shift their eyes to see the Charlotte that came before.

The evolution was relatively swift, as banks replaced mills, glass towered over brick, and asphalt blanketed dirt. In pockets, however, much of Charlotte's past has been reinvented as its future. In Uptown, in South End, and in the lives of over half a million Charlotteans, there are structures that remain, living a second life and serving a second purpose. It would be entirely appropriate to describe Charlotte itself in exactly that same way.

The town of Charlotte was incorporated in 1768. At that time, the Northeastern urban enclaves of New York, Philadelphia, and Boston could already claim their cityhood. In the 19th century, it was the port cities and railroad hubs of the Midwest—Chicago, St. Louis, and Cleveland—that staked their claims as major metropolitan centers, and if Los Angeles were in the Southeast, we would say it grew like kudzu. From just over 100,000 people in 1900, it was America's second largest city by century's end.

Charlotte, though taking great strides in the 20th century, seems to be making its move now. In 1990, it was ranked 33rd among American cities in population. Ten years later, it was 26th. By 2004, it was up to 20th. Tallying residents within the cities proper, it bypassed, among others, Denver, Seattle, and the aforementioned Boston in less than a decade and a half.

How exciting it must have been to witness the rise of Chicago or Los Angeles from virtually nothing. This generation of Charlotteans has the rare privilege of not only seeing but playing a role in a city's step to the fore. The reasons behind Charlotte's development have been researched, dissected, and described in other publications. It is not the purpose of this work to mine for the catalysts of Charlotte's emergence. Rather it is to document how Charlotte looked as it happened.

Notwithstanding the series title Then & Now, Charlotte is assembling girders so rapidly that it is virtually impossible for any documentation to be anything apart from Then & Then. Still that analysis should serve as cause to notice each addition, subtraction, and modification to the Queen City's appearance. A walking tour of Uptown shows that changes come almost daily. What readers will find here are the changes than came over a century. If it is true that to know where you came from is to know where you are going, then discover a place with eras and citizenries so diverse that only one word aptly describes them: American.

CHAPTER 1

UPTOWN BUILDINGS

THE RAZED, THE RESTORED, AND THE RISING

This is a view of Charlotte when it was arguably still a town. In 1904, this photograph was taken from the Tompkins Tower on South Church Street. Shown are South Tryon Street and much of Uptown Charlotte. In 1900, Charlotte's population was just over 18,000 residents. By 1910, the tally had nearly doubled, and it officially cracked 100,000 in 1940. The 2000 census counted well over half a million Charlotteans. The development of a city's skyline often appears proportional to a city's expansion as a whole. This chapter does much to make that case, as Charlotte and its center continue to grow outward and upward.

The Independence Building, shown here near its completion in 1908, was once the dominant figure on "the Square," the intersection of Trade and Tryon Streets. Opened in 1909 for the Charlotte visit of Pres. William Howard Taft, the Independence Building was North Carolina's first steel-frame skyscraper. Its original name was the Realty Building, but that was changed in 1912 when the Independence Trust Company was founded and occupied the ground floor. Two more stories were added in 1928, taking the tower to 14 floors. Notice the banner over Tryon Street advertising "Mecklenburg's Big Fair," offering flights on "Strobel's World Famous Air Ship." Despite efforts to save it, the Independence Building was imploded in 1981 to make way for the glistening and aptly named Independence Center.

Located on the west side of the 200 block of South Tryon Street, the Piedmont Building was built in the late 19th century and demolished in 1957. The photograph shown below is from the 1950s, shortly before the building's destruction. It originally housed the Piedmont Fire Insurance Company, whose name appeared above the ground-floor archway visible here. In 1902, the firm advertised "A company owned and operated by Charlotte people." Today this location is a construction site. Much of the space once occupied by the Piedmont has been earmarked for parking. The Johnston Building was to its right, and still stands today.

This steeple-like structure was Charlotte City Hall, located on the southeast corner of Fifth and Tryon Streets. Standing from 1891 to 1924, it was one of the few brownstone structures in town. This city hall featured a dragon weather vane and a clock that faced all four sides. Its appearance and the four-sided clock suggest that the architect, Gottfrid L. Norrman, may have been influenced by Philadelphia's signature city hall. This is pure speculation on the part of the author, though the similarities are striking. Today the North Carolina Blumenthal Performing Arts Center occupies the site. The Hearst Tower dominates the background.

Opened in 1902, the Trust Building stood at 210–212 South Tryon Street and housed the 1,350-seat Academy of Music. As indicated by the lettering across the building's front, the Trust Building was also home to the Catawba Power Company, organized in 1900 by South Carolina surgeon Dr. Gill Wylie. Wylie, engineer William States Lee, and tobacco magnate James Buchanan "Buck" Duke later founded the Southern Power Company. It was renamed Duke Power Company in 1935. The Trust Building was destroyed by fire in 1922. Its replacement, the Johnston Building, was built in 1924 and remains today.

Before this building was a hospital, it was a hotel. The Arlington Hotel—previously known as the Hotel Mecklenburg—occupied this structure on the southeast corner of Mint and Trade Streets. It was converted in 1903 after Presbyterian Hospital determined its previous facility to be too cramped. Another icon of Charlotte's ongoing sophistication will soon occupy this site: a 28-story condominium tower known as the TradeMark will soon cast its shadow on the Carillon Building, seen here on the left of the contemporary view.

Presbyterian Hospital, Charlotte, N. C.

NORTH GRADED SCHOOL
15034   CHARLOTTE, N.C.

The North School (or North Graded School, as indicated on this vintage postcard) opened in 1900 on Ninth Street between Brevard and Caldwell Streets. Designed by architect Frank Milburn, the North School survived until the 1970s. Today First Ward School occupies this block. The wall that parallels the sidewalk in the vintage view seems to have survived the old school's destruction. In the shadows of the tree, positioned in the center of the later view, is a large concrete patch filling the space once occupied by the steps to the North School.

Efird's Department Store, along with Belk and Ivey's, once anchored Uptown as a shopping destination. Shown here in the 1920s, Efird's was located at 120–126 North Tryon Street. To the left was city hall. To the right was the Alhambra Theatre, later the State Theatre. The Efird's chain was bought by Belk in 1956, but this store continued to operate as Efird's until 1959, when it too took the Belk name and became part of Belk's then-mammoth Uptown store. Now this site is occupied by none other than the signature of Charlotte's skyline, the Bank of America Corporate Center.

UPTOWN BUILDINGS

This was not the first Belk store, but it is arguably the store that launched a retail empire. The first Belk store opened in Monroe, North Carolina, in 1888. Belk's slogan for that initial establishment was "Cheap Goods Sell Themselves." Evidently by the time the Belk brothers opened their fourth store in 1895—shown here on Trade Street in Charlotte—customers needed to be reminded that Belk was the place for the frugal shopper. Notice the sign in the upper left reading "Cheapest Store on Earth." At this location today, there is a historical marker dedicated to Belk just to the left of the parking garage entrance. Above is the south side of Founder's Hall. As for Belk, there are now more than 220 stores in 14 states.

Ivey's Department Store at Fifth and Tryon Streets opened in 1924. Those who shopped here might remember that Mr. J. B. Ivey, a devout Methodist, provided a prayer room as well as a non-denominational chapel on the premises. What's more, no merchandise remotely associated with tobacco or alcohol usage was sold. Wine glasses could not be bought at Ivey's, nor was the color burgundy used in store advertising. The last of Charlotte's Uptown department stores closed in 1990 after Dillard's bought the Ivey's chain. Later the building was thought near demolition after voters rejected a bond issue that would have converted it into a magnet public high school. It did not, however, meet the wrecking ball, and today the building houses numerous businesses, townhouses, and offices, while still bearing Ivey's name.

Not to be confused with the Lawyers Building, which stood at 307 South Tryon Street, the Law Building was at 730 East Trade Street. It opened in 1929 and is shown here in the 1930s. Originally an eight-story structure, two more floors were added in 1967. It stood on the corner of Trade and Myers Streets. Myers is shown connecting through to Fourth Street. It no longer extends as such. Mecklenburg County Jail-Central now occupies several blocks on the south side of Trade, uninterrupted by cross streets.

Charlotte Sanatorium, Charlotte, N. C.

Located on the southeast corner of West Seventh and North Church Streets, the Charlotte Sanatorium was one of several small hospitals in Uptown Charlotte in early 20th century. It was organized in 1907 and closed in 1942. During World War II and after, the building took on a pair of patriotic functions. It was the Camp Sutton (Monroe, North Carolina) Station Hospital in 1943 and served as the regional office of the U.S. Veterans Administration into the early 1950s. At this corner today, one will find the rear of Discovery Place.

Charlotte, N. C.   North Carolina Medical College.

This pair of views brings three words immediately to mind: "It's still there!" The North Carolina Medical College building on the southeast corner of Sixth and North Church Streets was erected in 1907. The college, which existed from 1887 to 1914, was the only medical school for whites in North Carolina when this structure opened. The building later became the Pickler Hotel, among other functions, but its proximity to Old Settler's Cemetery undoubtedly led to its current name: Settler's Place. It now houses condominiums.

A 1985 *Charlotte Observer* article described the Addison Building as "never one of downtown's beauties." Still the structure at 222 South Church Street has avoided the wrecking ball by adjusting with the times. Built in 1928 as Charlotte's first multi-level parking facility, the Addison Garage underwent a complete overhaul in 1952–1953, when it was converted into an office building. Charlotte residents may remember energy-efficient green aluminum panels that enveloped the structure beginning in 1968. Those panels were removed in the mid-1980s as the Addison was once again remodeled, this time to a look reminiscent of its early days. Now a sign for Angry Ale's Restaurant adorns the building's façade. Perhaps not so coincidentally, a parking deck is right next door.

The modern Charlotte Chamber of Commerce can trace its roots to the Greater Charlotte Club founded in 1905. By the early 1920s, the chamber was located on the south side of West Fourth Street between Tryon and Church Streets, as shown here. It remained there until the early 1950s. W. E. Thomas Real Estate moved from its office in this 1920s view to the Johnston Building in 1931, where it did business until 1944. A modern structure with businesses facing both Tryon and Fourth Streets is there now. The pedestrian bridge to the right in the later view connects First Citizens Bank Tower with its parking deck.

On what had previously been a residential street, the Loose-Wiles Biscuit Company is shown in 1915, the year its Charlotte branch opened at 212 West First Street. Founded in Kansas City in 1902, Loose-Wiles used Sunshine Biscuits as its brand name and produced Hydrox Cookies among other snacks. Today it is a subsidiary of Keebler. The Charlotte branch of the company later moved to West Hill Street. Duke Energy now occupies the building on First Street in its revamped windowless form. It is ironic that the building that once marketed Sunshine is no longer open to it—architecturally speaking, of course.

Shown here in the 1920s, Shaw's Tire Store was on the southeast corner of Sixth and North College Streets. The business moved to Twenty-Seventh and North Tryon Streets in the 1950s. Notice the narrow tires, so different from modern tires, displayed in the window. Today this is a white-collar corner that shows no signs of its blue-collar past. The Holiday Inn Center City is located here at an angle with the corner itself. It stands directly across College Street from the Hearst Tower and diagonally across Sixth and College Streets from the Charlotte-Mecklenburg Library.

Facing dirt streets and crumbling curbs in this 1911 photograph, the Mecklenburg Auto Company was once located at 211 South Church Street. Mecklenburg Auto later moved to West Fifth Street. The Burwell-Walker Company, in the automobile business as well, later occupied this site. Burwell-Walker sold Dort, Chalmers, and Oldsmobile models until 1921. That firm later relocated to North Tryon Street and was renamed Burwell-Harris Company. A parking garage now stands on the Church Street site.

In 1988, *The Charlotte Observer* called this "Charlotte's most frequently renamed building." When it opened in 1927, the initial moniker of the 20-story tower at 112 South Tryon Street was the First National Bank Building. By 1932, it was the Liberty Life Building, a title it retained for 31 years. Then it was renamed the Baugh Building after its owner. It has also been known as First Southeastern Center and the Bank of North Carolina Building, among other names. The name is not all that has changed. Once the tallest building in North Carolina, 112 Tryon Plaza—its name in 2005—is now not even the tallest building on its block. Still standing as one of the few holdovers from Tryon Street's previous life, perhaps its next name should be the Bastion.

The vintage view shown here is a postcard depicting the YMCA and Latta Arcade at the northwest corner of Second and Tryon Streets *c.* 1920. The YMCA building was built in 1908 and demolished in 1960. Today the building housing the Charlotte Chamber of Commerce occupies that corner. The two-story building to the right of the YMCA is Latta Arcade. Opened in 1915, it was designed by architect William H. Peeps, who also designed the Ivey's Department Store building at Fifth and Tryon. Latta Arcade remains today and, though shielded by trees, is visible in the contemporary view.

In 1999, the entire block on the east side of Tryon Street between First and Second Streets was demolished except for the building that housed Ratcliffe's Flowers. It was moved to the other side of Tryon for months then moved back and incorporated into a new mixed-use building. Today it can be seen with the signature hanging sign it has displayed for decades as an integral element of the high-rise that now stands at 435 South Tryon. The original structure was designed by architect William H. Peeps, who also designed Latta Arcade and the Ivey's Department Store building.

Sears Roebuck and Company is not to be ignored when remembering Uptown Charlotte's retail past. Built in 1927, this building on the southwest corner of Third and Tryon Streets also housed Brown's Incorporated, a clothing store; Haverty's Furniture; and in the 1980s, Jack Wood Limited, a men's clothing store. A parking lot now occupies the site. The Esso station on the northwest corner (the near corner as shown) is long gone. The office building there today was experiencing an ongoing conversion in 2005. It will house condominiums under the name 230 South Tryon scheduled to open in the summer of 2006.

UPTOWN BUILDINGS

The Carolina Theatre at Sixth and Tryon Streets was Charlotte's last movie palace. It is pictured here in 1931 when showing Buster Keaton in *Parlor, Bedroom, and Bath*. More than a movie theatre, the Carolina originally had 1,450 seats, was also a playhouse, and hosted live acts including Elvis Presley and Frank Sinatra. Closed in 1978 and damaged by fire started by vagrants in 1980, it is now owned by the city. Its storefront façade on Tryon was removed in 2005 and will be incorporated into a new residential high-rise on the site. The theatre itself remains and, as it has always been, is set back from the sidewalk along Tryon. The Carolina Theatre Preservation Society plans to restore and reopen the theatre with 1,200 seats.

The Professional Building housed exactly what the name suggests—medical professionals. Built in 1923 on the northwest corner of Seventh and Tryon Streets, this structure is classic 1920s American urbanity. The cars on the street, the office identification lettering directly on the window glass, and its anchoring of the corner create a sense that the Professional Building would have been just as congruent with Roaring-Twenties Chicago as burgeoning Charlotte. It was demolished in 1995 and replaced by TransAmerica Square. Today this corner includes the popular nightspots Rock Bottom Brewery and Therapy.

CHAPTER 2

STREETS

Trade, Tryon, and Travels around Town

This image, looking south on College Street from Fourth Street *c.* 1904, is highly representative of the look to "Off-Tryon" Uptown in this era. A small remnant of the sign for Durham and Klueppelburg Grocery Company can be seen in the upper left corner of this image. More conspicuous to its right is B. D. Springs and Company at 205 South College Street. The nearest sign on the right side of the street, at 202, is for B. F. Withers, dealing in building material and feed.

This is the northwest corner of Trade and Tryon, known in the 19th and early 20th centuries as Old Osborne Corner. The building square with the corner housed Woodall and Sheppard Drugstore. That company later occupied a ground floor space in the Realty (Independence) Building after its 1909 completion on this site.

The Selwyn Hotel is visible to the far left of this view, almost certainly dating this image to 1907, the year the Selwyn opened, and the year before the Realty Building's construction took over this corner. Independence Center occupies this block of the Square today.

This is Trade and Tryon Streets. It is Charlotte's signature corner, the Square. About the only thing that remains the same from 1955 until today is that motorists cannot make turns onto Trade from Tryon. Efird's Department Store is on the right, Ivey's Department Store is visible on the left, and Liggett Drugs is front and center; this was a classic 1950s Main Street. Despite the active presence of performing arts on this block, there is a sterility here that is much more corporate than cultural. Tree-lined streets, skyscrapers, and sculpture are all very nice indeed, but it is the WBT microphone billboard and the big Coca-Cola sign on the drugstore that people will remember.

A trolley is shown traveling on Tryon Street. This view of Tryon looks north from Third Street *c.* 1905. If the trolley is traveling south, it has just passed the Buford Hotel, shown on the right at the northeast corner of Tryon and Fourth Streets. It is about to pass the YMCA, visible on the left with the cone-shaped turret. It will finally pass the Trust Building, the nearest building shown on the left. The Johnston Building, which occupies the site of the old Trust Building, is on the near left of the modern view.

In 1952, West First Street between Church and Mint Streets was teeming with commercial life. In the foreground on the left of the vintage view is Shaw Distributing Company. According to Charlotte city directories, Shaw dealt in wholesale radios and refrigerators. Today the building on the right appears to be a revamping of the structure in the vintage view. Both sides of this block of First Street are now Duke Energy properties.

In the late 19th century, R. M. White Ind. Company was a wholesale and retail grocer on East Trade Street near College Street. The building next door, on the corner, was later occupied by the Bee Hive. To the left of R. M. White but not shown was the building that housed Belk's first Charlotte store. Despite the interesting architecture in view, one cannot help but be drawn to the man with his face in the shadows. He appears set for a Trade Street shootout. Today the south façade of Founder's Hall marks this site's tamer atmosphere.

This is Fourth Street looking west from its intersection with College Street. The change is obvious. Every structure appearing in the vintage view is long gone. The pedestrian bridge in the modern view, part of the Overstreet Mall, connects the Bank of America Plaza Parking Garage and the Omni Hotel with the BB&T Center at 200 South College Street. What remains the same is evident when you visit this location. Despite is proximity to the epicenter of Uptown business and social life, this is a relatively barren side street. It has few storefronts, and pedestrian traffic is nearly absent. It would seem that it has always been that way.

Notwithstanding the passage of time, it is difficult to believe that each of these views depicts the same site. In this 1904 view looking north at College Street from just south of East Fourth Street, the most visible business from Charlotte's past is the Durham and Klueppelberg Grocery Company. The Philip Carey Manufacturing Company, which dealt in roofing material, is seen on the left. The shorter building toward the center of the view on the right side of the street was the Textile Mill Supply Company, demolished in the early 1920s. This location experienced a recent demolition as well: the old Charlotte Convention Center met its demise in 2005, leaving behind a pedestrian bridge that, at the time of publication, remained a bridge to nothing.

Before Efird's blossomed into a 58-store chain throughout the Carolinas, the Efird brothers' initial enterprise was the Bee Hive at 43–47 East Trade Street on the northwest corner of College Street. This image is looking north on College from Trade. Its formal name was the Charlotte Mercantile Company. In 1907, the title Efird's Department Store was adopted. Neither the Bee Hive nor any of the other brick buildings in view survive today. The southeast side of Founder's Square is on this corner now.

These images suggest that someone forgot to take down the Ratcliffe's Flowers sign—no such mistake was made. The sign hangs today for Ratcliffe's on the Green, a restaurant and wine room. Other signs are long gone from the east side of Tryon Street looking north here from First Street. Loo Ling Laundry was at 433 South Tryon Street. Ratcliffe's was at 431. Johnston's Furniture Company was at 425–427. The lower five letters of Johnston's sign are in view. In the distance on the right are the Johnston Building and the Liberty Life Building. Both still stand but are blocked from view at this site today. In the modern image, the base of Three Wachovia Center is on the right. 400 South Tryon Street is on the left.

Recreating the precise vantage point of this 1950s photograph proved impossible due to more recent construction in the area. Still this pair of views does much to illustrate the changes to this locale. Looking west across Tryon Street between Second and Third Streets, Latta Arcade is all that remains. Shown in the center of the contemporary view, Latta Arcade is toward the left of the 1950s image. The parking lot is long gone, and much of that space was a construction site at the time of publication for the reopening of Wachovia Main, scheduled for 2006. The construction zone displayed an outdoor gallery of photographs of the vicinity over the years.

Like most blocks Uptown, almost nothing remains from the past at this one. This is West Trade Street looking west past its intersection with Church Street. On the right is the Selwyn Hotel. Marriott City Center is there today. On the left of the 1960s view is the Piedmont Restaurant at 201–203 West Trade. New York Cleaners and Hatters is also visible at 215 West Trade Street. The large building on the left is the Hotel Charlotte. All those businesses on the south side of Trade Street are gone; the Carillon Building now stands in their place. All that remains constant at this intersection is First Presbyterian Church. It is on the northwest corner and out of view both then and now.

This is Trade Street looking east from Brevard Street toward Caldwell Avenue. Though Tryon Street has always been Charlotte's version of Main Street, this section of Trade Street had all the characteristics defining the term: two-way traffic with myriad shops and eateries convenient to pedestrians. Today it is a much different scene, but it is a destination once again. Where once patrons of small business came by day, sports fans now come by night. The brand new Charlotte Bobcats Arena dominates the left side of the street. The building is also home to the Charlotte Sting and Charlotte Checkers.

The building that dominates this late 1950s photograph is Charlotte Police Headquarters, seen on the right at the corner of East Fourth and Alexander Streets. The police department, identified by its neon sign, was headquartered here from 1925 to 1969 before moving to Fourth and McDowell Streets. None of the small structures on the left remain. Today the Charlotte-Mecklenburg Government Center is on that side of the street. Virtually all of the Charlotte skyline shown here has been erected since the earlier photograph was taken.

Unless one had an intimate knowledge of this block, it would be nearly impossible to match the locale of these images. This is looking east on Fourth Street toward Myers Street, where virtually nothing but the contour of the pavement has survived the five-plus decades since the 1950s photograph was snapped. Even Myers Street itself no longer crosses Fourth. Its former path is now occupied by the Mecklenburg County Jail-Central, shown here on the left. On the right is the brand-new Mecklenburg County Courthouse, still in a state of construction.

If one wishes to visit Charlotte's quaint Fourth Ward, here is a path to get there. This is the 700 block of North Graham Street looking south toward West Tenth Street. Hart's Cleaners, shown on the right, was at 727 North Graham Street. Shown well beyond Hart's is Bank's Amoco Station. The building now on the corner of Tenth and Graham is 626 North Graham condominiums. The Garrison at Graham condominiums will soon be built adjacent to the scaffolding on the right. If one stood from the point of view of the modern image, their back would virtually be against Interstate 277.

The vintage view looking east on East Sixth Street from its intersection with Davidson Street dates to the era when dirt streets could still be found in Charlotte's four wards. Unpaved streets still existed in Charlotte's central areas into the late 1940s. The contemporary view of this block speaks volumes about the evolution Charlotte has experienced. The houses that lined this block are long gone, and the street is now open to one-way traffic only. Notice as well the short Davidson Street signpost on the corner versus the overhead signs that label Charlotte streets today.

The early view of West Trade Street at its intersection with Tuckaseegee Road is a veritable collage of 1940s style. The Esso service station, the billboard for Nesbitt's soda, and the mingling of cars with horse-drawn wagons all serve to illustrate the contrast between the look of the mid-20th century and that of the early 21st. Today the traffic pattern at this corner has been altered. The Citgo station in the modern view now sits where eastbound traffic once continued onto Trade Street. One structure that remains from then to now is the white industrial building at the top of the hill on Trade Street. Interstate 77 commuters may notice that this intersection is visible from the southbound lanes of the highway.

These views depict North Tryon Street looking south from its intersection with Dalton Avenue. Notice the Esso gas station on the corner. When Standard Oil was broken up into seven regional companies, Standard Oil of New Jersey won the rights to the Standard brand in several states, including North Carolina. It used the name Esso, a derivative of Standard Oil's initials. Standard Oil Company of New Jersey renamed itself Exxon Corporation in 1974 and adopted that name throughout the United States. Today the one common thread between this corner's past and present is the Exxon station that stands where the Esso station once operated.

In the late 1940s and early 1950s, motorists traveling northeast on Dalton Avenue toward North Tryon Street would see a lot of boxcars straight ahead. The tracks are still there, as are plenty of boxcars sitting idle, but one would have to do a little looking to find them now. Blocking the sight line that once existed is a business known as Extravaganza, which rents themed decor for business parties. This site is just south of the Amtrak passenger station on North Tryon Street.

The construction of Interstate 277 created a good deal of confusion after the fact for anyone attempting to locate certain places by the addresses they once used. Many streets and roads in Charlotte simply do not go where they used to go. This pair of views is an excellent example.

Shown here is what was once Independence Boulevard curving past Caldwell Street and heading toward Morehead Street. Independence no longer connects directly to Uptown. Today this is an extension of Stonewall Street, while a turn to the left puts motorists on Interstate 277.

The general store shown here at Third and Graham Streets is long gone. Massive changes came to Charlotte's Third Ward with the construction of Bank of America Stadium (formerly Ericsson Stadium) and its need for nearby parking. Still this corner will always be remembered for one of Charlotte's best-known criminal capers. On November 15, 1933, the Chicago-based "Touhy Gang" used machine guns to hold up a mail truck at this site and made off with $120,000. The group was later nabbed after a ripped-up laundry ticket traced to Chicago was found near the scene. The sign on the corner today forecasts more change. It reads, "Coming soon, the new West Park in Third Ward."

STREETS

This is East Seventh Street looking west from its corner with Pecan Avenue (right). The scene showing Stanley's Cut-Rate Drugs is from the 1950s. Stanley's remained until 1998. The building lives on and houses Schlotzsky's Deli, a Starbucks, and a comic book shop named Heroes Aren't Hard to Find. Dollar General is in a building beyond and out of view. Set back a bit from the corner of Seventh and Caswell Streets at left, where the Pure gas station once stood, is a bar named the Philosopher's Stone. It is partially visible through the trees.

The vintage view shown here should be recognizable by its traffic pattern alone. This is Morehead Street looking east toward its intersection with McDowell Street (on the left) and Dilworth Road (veering to the right). Like many other images in this volume, a classic filling station is shown. The Atlantic station on the right once operated where today one will find Art's BBQ and Deli as well as an H&R Block office. The steeple dominating the contemporary view is that of Covenant Presbyterian Church.

This is Cecil Street looking north toward Seventh Street in the 1950s. Cecil is now North Kings Drive. Kings Drive becomes Central Avenue north of Seventh. The same was true of Cecil Street. Winkler's Kayo service station, known at times as the Kayo Oil Company, was located at 401 Central Avenue. A small patch of woods separating Seventh from Independence Boulevard is there now. The sign for Bob's Esso station is visible on the left, but the station itself was behind the billboards. In the modern image of this location, it is apparent that the street has been widened significantly. The houses are gone, and the Grady Cole Center is now on the right.

This is the intersection of South Boulevard and East Bland Street *c.* 1950. Henry's service station, shown here on the left, no longer stands. What has survived is the old trolley barn. By the time this vintage photograph was taken, that building, shown here on the right, had been converted to the Duke Power Company bus garage. Notice the bus pulling out of its stall to enter the roadway. Today three sides of the building remain. The back wall is gone, exposing the structure's interior, clearly visible when traveling east on Bland Street toward South Boulevard.

BUSINESS

THINGS MADE, THINGS SOLD, AND THINGS OLD

This is Roland Ferguson, a driver for Sanitary Steam Laundry, standing by his truck parked on North Cecil Street (now Kings Drive). Notice the three-digit phone numbers for the company on the truck's side. The business was located at 1407 South Boulevard and was owned by Charles R. Price. Ferguson, shown here around 1920, had by 1925 taken a job as a salesman for the Pepsi-Cola Bottling Company. In this chapter, the reader will find stories both human and commercial.

This is the Charlotte Oil and Fertilizer Company around 1900. Owned by D. A. Tompkins, who also built and owned Atherton Mill, this company was later known as the Southern Cotton Oil Company. Its location in relation to Atherton Mill was on the other side of what are now the trolley tracks in South End. A comparison of maps of the era with modern maps suggests that Hawkins Street, shown in the foreground of the contemporary view, was extended. The aforementioned comparison also suggests that this section of Hawkins Street, shown in front of another early-20th-century industrial building, now cuts its path through the site once occupied by Charlotte Oil and Fertilizer.

Atherton Cotton Mill opened in 1893 in the area of town now known as South End. It was built and owned by Daniel Augustus Tompkins, whose industrial influence in the South cannot be done justice in the space provided here. Atherton Mill continued to operate until the 1930s, until it was acquired by the J. Schoenith Company and converted to candy production. Motorists traveling south from Uptown on South Boulevard today will still see the mill's smokestack directly ahead. Located behind South End Brewery, the building is now divided into commercial and residential lofts named quite simply Atherton Lofts.

Fig. 21. Atherton Cotton Mills.

Located at 200–206 East Bland Street, Wiggins Brothers, pictured here in 1923, dealt in lumber and building materials. According to Charlotte city directories, myriad businesses bearing the Wiggin's name occupied all or part of this property until 1967. Standard Sales Company occupied the site in 1933. Identifying its business as building material, it might be presumed to be the same company under a temporary name. Greek Isles restaurant occupies the space today. Around the far corner and in connection is Jillian's, a popular South End nightspot. The building's exterior has changed little over time. Doors and windows remain where they have always been. The same can be said of the telephone pole on the corner and even the fire hydrant to the pole's left.

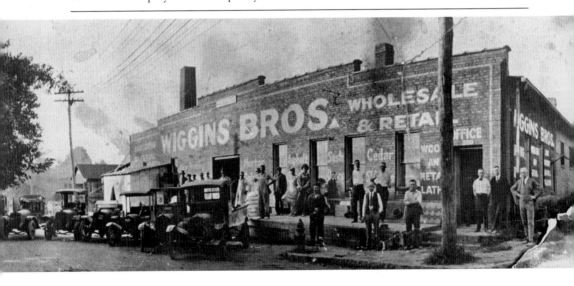

Charlotte Pipe and Foundry Company was founded in 1901 by Willis Frank Dowd. The company's original plant was located at the corner of South Boulevard and Park Avenue. That facility was destroyed by fire in 1907. A replacement plant was built on South Clarkson Street and is shown here under construction. Charlotte Pipe and Foundry is still a private, family-owned business today. It continues to operate at the Clarkson Street location. A pair of W. Frank Dowd's great-grandsons runs the company now. Roddey Dowd Jr. is president, while Frank Dowd IV is CEO and chairman of the board.

The Woodall and Sheppard Drug Store was the result of a partnership that dated to the postgraduate days of the proprietors. J. P. Woodall and J. W. Sheppard were classmates at Philadelphia College of Pharmacy. Following graduation, the duo went to Memphis, and four years later, they came to Charlotte to set up shop. They bought the Reese and Robinson Drug Store on the corner of Trade and Tryon Streets. Upon the completion of the Realty Building (Independence Building) on the Square, the business moved into the ground floor shop shown here at 9 North Tryon Street. Today several storefront businesses operate on this site where Independence Center now stands.

This pair of views represents America then and now as much as it does Charlotte. Shown is the interior of Woodall and Sheppard Drug Store, which faced Tryon Street, c. 1910. Located on the ground floor of the Independence Building on the northwest corner of the Square, this image could easily be mistaken for a shop in any American town's antique district. The glass showcases, the elegant fixtures, even the packaging of the articles for sale combined to give a business as mundane as a drug store sophistication. Independence Center now occupies this corner. The interior of one of its ground-floor businesses facing Tryon Street is shown as well—Starbucks.

This massive building on Statesville Avenue, opened in 1925, is shown around the time of its completion. It was erected as a Ford assembly plant. During World War II, it was sold to the government and converted into a quartermaster depot, supplying military installations in the Carolinas. Following the war, it was used to house the remains of over 5,000 dead servicemen before being returned to their families in the Carolinas and other neighboring states. Later it functioned as a missile assembly plant for Douglas Aircraft Company. Today it is part of a three-building complex comprising a distribution center for Eckerd Drug.

Haralson and Grice Service Station No. 2 opened for business on the northwest corner of Morehead and Mint Streets in 1927. The enterprise used the same name for its station at Mint and Bland Streets from 1924 to 1926. The station shown changed its name to Grice Keely Company in 1929. Today this corner is the base of a pair of Interstate 277 overpasses. Bank of America Stadium is in the background.

According to the 1955 *Charlotte City Directory*, Bob's Esso service station stood at 1106 East Seventh Street. Notice the billboard advertising a brand new Nash for $1,550. This corner has changed so much its barely recognizable. The corner was once the intersection of Seventh and Cecil Streets. Today it is the corner of Seventh Street and North Kings Drive, where Central Avenue becomes North Kings Drive. Now a vacant lot used by day for parking, the only remnant that carries over from the past is a small part of a retaining wall. Now crumbling, the wall in its complete form is visible to the left of the Esso station in front of the Nash billboard. The homes on each side of station are gone as well.

Here's one establishment that has adapted with and survived the massive changes Charlotte has seen since this photograph was snapped in the 1950s. At the corner of South Independence Boulevard and East Fourth Street, Jerry's Drive-In later changed its name to the Town and Country Drive-In. In 1969, it became the Athens Restaurant, which is open to this day. While the Athens' perseverance is remarkable, what is downright amazing is the career of one of its employees, Annie McLean. Annie, an African American woman, took a job here in 1963 when it was still a whites-only establishment. Starting as a cook, Annie shifted to waiting tables in the early 1970s and still does so today!

This *c.* 1949 image shows Myers Park Pharmacy on East Morehead Street in the foreground and the Mecklenburg County Market on Harding Place in the background. The pharmacy has long since disappeared, but in its day, it featured a soda fountain and delivered prescriptions on three-wheel motorcycles. The Mecklenburg County Market lives on. To the right in the contemporary view, it has been open continuously since 1938 and is thought to be the oldest farmers' market in North Carolina. Originally on Trade Street, it was founded by a group of 13 ladies known as the Mecklenburg County Home Demonstration Club. Some of the current members of the co-op are descendants of the original 13.

CHAPTER 4

HOTELS

WASHINGTON SLEPT HERE

The Gem Restaurant was part of the Central Hotel. The Gem included a dining room, a banquet hall, and the lunchroom, shown here in the early 20th century. An advertisement in the 1902 *Charlotte City Directory* characterized the lunchroom as the "best in the city. Open all night. Best conducted lunch counter in the state." A display case containing cigars is visible on the left. Fruit is stacked at both the near and far ends of the counter.

73

The Central Hotel, shown around 1900, was on the southeast corner of the Square. Known in other eras as Sadler's Hotel and the Mansion House, the Central was reportedly once the largest hotel between Richmond and Atlanta. Prior to his marriage, Henry Belk boarded here, across Trade Street from his first Charlotte store. The Central became the Albert Hotel in 1931. From 1942 to 1973, an S. H. Kress five-and-dime store occupied the site, which later became Bank of America Plaza. Today it continues to be a corporate enclave. The Omni Hotel on the left of the contemporary view maintains the corner's inn-keeping tradition.

The Queen City Hotel once occupied the northeast corner of Fifth and College Streets. Looking at the vintage view, it was the left half that was the original hotel, the right half of the structure being added later. Known also as the Hotel Dixie in 1921, the hotel reassumed the Queen City name in 1922 and featured the Kentucky Dining Room. Later the Walton Hotel occupied this site, standing until the 1950s. Today the Trade Center, subtitled Charlotte's International Trade Center, occupies this corner.

The Leland Hotel, shown here around 1904, was completed in 1900 at 227 North Tryon Street. According to Charlotte city directories, it was later known as the Tryon Hotel. Notice the people on the second-floor balcony overlooking North Tryon Street. The site has since been restored to a style reminiscent of its previous look. On the left today is a restaurant and bar called Zink. CVS Pharmacy is in the center, and Monticello Uptown Restaurant and Bar is on the right. The Dunhill Hotel (formerly the Mayfair Hotel) is on the corner to the far right.

Closed in 1970 after its owners decided it was not worth necessary refurbishments, the Clayton Hotel met its demise after 60 years at the northeast corner of Church and Fifth Streets. Far from an upscale establishment at the end, full-time residents paid $60 a month to call it home. The expense of living at this site is certainly about to change. The corner will soon give rise to a new, sparkling condominium tower known as Avenue. Among its planned features is a 10th-floor pool and sundeck. In the contemporary view provided here, the side of Latorre's Latin American restaurant remains visible on the right.

HOTELS

This is the 200 block of the south side of West Trade Street around 1930. The Hotel Charlotte, opened in 1924, was the dominant feature of this block. Just as New England Inns might boast "Washington slept here," the Hotel Charlotte could advertise to both sides of the 20th-century political spectrum. Franklin Roosevelt and Richard Nixon each slept here (Washington did visit Charlotte in 1791 and spent the night at an inn on West Trade Street.) In 1961, it became the Queen Charlotte Hotel. It was the White House Inn when it closed in 1973—coincidentally, a year just as tough for its more recent White House guest. Despite the hotel's status on the National Register of Historic Places, it was imploded in 1988. In its place today is the Carillon Building.

At the northeast corner of Trade and Church Streets stood the Selwyn Hotel. Shown here on an early-20th-century postcard, the Selwyn was opened in 1907, remodeled in 1948, and closed in 1964. Its advertising was typical for American hotels of the era. Early on, it boasted electric lights in 75 of its 150 rooms and telephones and running water in every room. In the first half of the 20th century, it was also common for hotels to advertise their buildings as fireproof. This essentially meant that the building was of masonry rather than wooden construction. The Selwyn touted its status as the "first fireproof hotel in North Carolina." Today the west end of the Marriott City Center occupies this corner.

The Hotel Selwyn, Charlotte, N. C.

The Traveler's Hotel stood at 533 West Trade Street as late as 1994. The reverse side of the vintage postcard shown, which dates to the 1950s or perhaps late 1940s, advertises "inner-spring mattresses and electric fans" in the hotel's rooms. The card also boasts a "sanitary rating of 96%."

Less than a block from the Southern Railway station, it was nonetheless a longer walk for train passengers than the Stonewall Hotel, which stood right next door to the Traveler's. Today the site is a parking lot.

TRAVELER'S HOTEL. 533 WEST TRADE STREET, CHARLOTTE, N. C.

CHAPTER

HOMES

LOCATION, LOCATION, LOCATION

RESIDENCE OF H. A. KLUEPPELBURG.

This is the *c.* 1905 home of Henry A. Klueppelburg at 415 South Tryon Street, on the corner with First Street. The Klueppelburg name was associated with a pair of Uptown businesses in early-20th-century Charlotte. The Durham and Klueppelburg Grocery Company is shown on page 42. Klueppelburg was also associated with H. A. Cook and Company at 418 North A Street. North A Street later became Brevard Street. H. A. Cook's business was bagged and tied cotton bales.

While Uptown Charlotte is currently experiencing a residential resurgence, homes in the heart of town were once typically like those shown here. In congruence with Charlotte's growth from town to city, the taste of Uptown's upper crust has shifted from stately to urbane, high-rise condominiums now being the rage. This Greek revival–style house at 801 North Tryon was built in the late 19th century and was home to attorney C. W. Tillett. This corner was later occupied by an A&P grocery store, which closed in 1975. Today a shoe and clothing store does business on the site. Just beyond the shrubbery on the right side of the modern view is Interstate 277.

There was a time when the corporate corridor that is North Tryon Street was largely residential. The Latta Johnston House, shown here around 1920, was at 609 North Tryon Street. Latta C. Johnston, a stock farmer for whom this home continued to be known, was deceased by 1893. The building formerly known as the Manger Motor Inn, home to Hearth and Embers Restaurant and now known as Renaissance Place Apartments, is on this site today.

The five-block stretch of East Trade Street running from Brevard Street to McDowell Street was known for a time as East Avenue. This home at 804 East Avenue (another source shows the address as 812) belonged to John S. "Jack" Myers. Notice the children on the front steps. The homeowner was also a landowner. In the early 20th century. Myers's plantation was developed into Charlotte's Myers Park neighborhood by his son-in-law, George Stephens. East Avenue later reverted to the East Trade Street name, and the site of the Myers house is now occupied by Mecklenburg County Jail-Central.

These views depict West Fifth Street's 900 block looking toward Irwin Avenue. In the late 1940s view, the large house on the right, at 912 West Fifth Street, is that of Harriet Morrison-Irwin. Morrison-Irwin is known for her 1869 patent of a hexagonal house design, and a part of the house visible here does have a hexagonal shape. Mrs. Morrison-Irwin was a sister of Mrs. Stonewall Jackson, Mary Anna Morrison, whose home stood just a few blocks away and is also shown in this volume. Today Post Corporate Apartments occupies the site adjacent to Gateway Village and Johnson and Wales University.

Contrary to what this vintage postcard indicates, Gen. Stonewall Jackson not only did not reside in this home, he never lived in Charlotte. This is the home of Mrs. Stonewall Jackson. Known as the "First Lady of Charlotte," Jackson's widow, Mary Anna Morrison, was born in Charlotte in 1831.

Following her husband's death and after a stint in Lincoln County, Mrs. Jackson returned to her hometown and resided in this house at 507 West Trade Street. The Stonewall Hotel later occupied the site, and today it is a parking lot with Bank of America Stadium now visible in the distance.

Thad Tate was one of early Charlotte's leading African American citizens. Born in 1865, the same year as the Civil War's conclusion, Tate worked in Charlotte as a barber for 61 years beginning in 1882. He owned the shop in the Central Hotel. Among the numerous civic positions held by Tate, he was treasurer of the Brevard Street Library for Negroes. His home, shown here, was located in First Ward at 508 (504 in some documents) East Seventh Street. The brick home is long gone, and another brick structure is in its place today. Shown is the back of the Autumn Place Living Center.

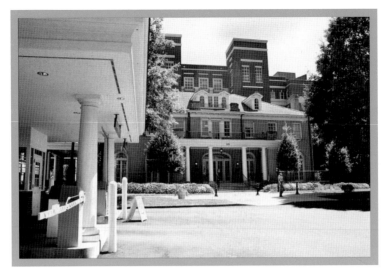

The W. H. Belk Mansion on Hawthorne Lane was built in 1923 for the department-store magnate. William Henry Belk chaired the board of Presbyterian Hospital for many years, and the Belk family is a longtime benefactor. The home, located on the hospital campus, was donated to the hospital in 1968 following the death of W. H. Belk's widow, Mary Irwin. In 1990, the 1,100-ton house was moved 150 feet closer to the hospital to make room for the construction of a six-level parking deck. It is shown here today on the hospital grounds, adjacent to the parking deck it accommodated.

Mid-rise apartment buildings were common on North Church Street and in Fourth Ward beginning in the 1920s and the 1930s. The Jefferson is no exception. At 409 North Church Street near the corner with West Seventh Street, the Jefferson stood until the 1990s. Before its demolition, the engraved Jefferson lettering, as well as the canopy over its front door, were removed, and now, bridging past and present, adorn the residences of Jefferson Square on this site.

Though it has experienced some modifications, this structure remains today. The H. D. Dennis Apartment Building is at the corner of Hopedale and Granville Roads near Queens Road West. The vintage photograph evidently was taken during the building's construction in the late 1920s. The parapets that once traced the roofline are gone, leaving the even roofline seen today. The staggered brick window planters remain and are put to use by the current residents. The building is now known as Granville Place Condominiums.

CHAPTER 6

TRANSPORTATION

THE COMINGS AND GOINGS
OF COMING AND GOING

The throngs of Charlotteans shown on the Square assembled to witness the last trolley ride on March 14, 1938. Electric streetcar operation in Charlotte began in 1893. Streetcar No. 85, built in the trolley barn that partially remains on South Boulevard, made the farewell trip from Presbyterian Hospital to the Square and then home to the trolley barn for retirement. Though trolleys no longer grace the intersection of Trade and Tryon Streets as pictured here, No. 85 has been restored and returned to service.

The first passenger train arrived in Charlotte on the Charlotte and South Carolina Railroad in 1852. That railroad was later acquired by the Richmond and Danville Railroad, which was absorbed by the Southern Railway System in 1894. Shown here is traffic halted as a passenger train crosses West Trade Street next to the Southern Railway Station. Though one will still find tracks crossing at street level elsewhere in Charlotte, there are no longer such delays here. Rail traffic, such as the freight train shown hauling trailers, now passes over Trade Street.

The Southern Railway Station on West Trade Street, designed by architect Frank Milburn, was built in 1905 and lasted until 1963. It replaced a passenger station of the Richmond and Danville Railroad on the same site. That line was absorbed by the Southern Railway System.

The 1905 station, shown here with a parking lot full of 1950s cars, was within a block of both the Stonewall and Traveler's Hotels, each designed by Milburn as well. Still a center for transportation, a Greyhound bus depot now operates at this location.

The Seaboard Air Line Railroad Passenger Terminal was opened in 1896. The railroad later changed its name to the Seaboard Coast Line. The terminal replaced an earlier station that burned in 1895, and it remains today at 945 North College Street, just north of Interstate 277. Easily seen from North Tryon Street, it is now known as the Urban Ministries Center and provides a soup kitchen and other services for the homeless. Over 600 individuals receive their mail here. With the construction of a new and adjacent soup kitchen, the station will become Artwork 945 beginning in 2006, its mission being to provide the homeless with access to culture. Much of the old station's interior is now adorned with the artwork of the homeless people it has served.

This is Thomas B. Hoover at the reigns of one of his horse-drawn buggies in front of the livery stable displaying his name. One source indicates that T. B. Hoover and Company was located at 223 East Trade Street, though the address over the door clearly indicates 233 East Trade as the location. By 1911, that address changed to 239. The image shown here is from 1905. Facing Trade Street on this site today is the side of the parking deck that sits between Founder's Hall (across College Street) and the new Charlotte Bobcats Arena.

Across America, People are Discovering Something Wonderful. *Their Heritage.*

Arcadia Publishing is the leading local history publisher in the United States. With more than 3,000 titles in print and hundreds of new titles released every year, Arcadia has extensive specialized experience chronicling the history of communities and celebrating America's hidden stories, bringing to life the people, places, and events from the past. To discover the history of other communities across the nation, please visit:

www.arcadiapublishing.com

Customized search tools allow you to find regional history books about the town where you grew up, the cities where your friends and family live, the town where your parents met, or even that retirement spot you've been dreaming about.